PHONICS Workbook

LEVEL 1

Published in Moonstone
by Rupa Publications India Pvt. Ltd 2022
7/16, Ansari Road, Daryaganj
New Delhi 110002

Sales centres:
Allahabad Bengaluru Chennai
Hyderabad Jaipur Kathmandu
Kolkata Mumbai

Copyright © Rupa Publications India Pvt. Ltd 2022

The views and opinions expressed in this book are
the authors' own and the facts are as reported by them
which have been verified to the extent possible,
and the publishers are not in any way liable for the same.

All rights reserved.
No part of this publication may be reproduced, transmitted,
or stored in a retrieval system, in any form or by any means,
electronic, mechanical, photocopying, recording or otherwise,
without the prior permission of the publisher.

P-ISBN: 978-93-5520-646-6
E-ISBN: 978-93-5520-647-3

First impression 2022

10 9 8 7 6 5 4 3 2 1

The moral right of the authors has been asserted.

Printed in India
This book is sold subject to the condition that it shall not,
by way of trade or otherwise, be lent, resold, hired out, or otherwise
circulated, without the publisher's prior consent, in any form of binding
or cover other than that in which it is published.

Contents

An Angry Ant 4	A Talking Toy 27
A Baked Bun 5	Learn More 28
A Colourful Cap 6	The Unique Unicorn 29
A Dainty Duck 7	A Vegetable Van 30
Learn More 8	A Wally Walrus 31
An Easter Egg 9	A Xylophone 32
A Foolish Fox 10	A Yellow Yo-Yo 33
A Good Goat 11	A Zesty Zebra 34
A Happy Hen 12	Learn More 35
Learn More 13	Learn More 36
An Icy Igloo 14	Rhyme Time 37
A Jolly Joey 15	Matching Fun 38
A Kind King 16	Beginning Letter's Sound 39
A Loving Lion 17	Beginning Sound 40
Learn More 18	Final Sound 41
The Magical Moon 19	Beginning and Final Sounds 42
A Noble Nurse 20	Picture Reading 43
An Old Owl 21	Read and Colour 44
A Playful Pup 22	Fun at the Zoo 45
Learn More 23	Fun with Fruits 46
A Quiet Queen 24	Fun with Animals 47
A Red Rose 25	Word Ladder 48
Smelly Socks 26	

An Angry Ant

Trace and write the letters and the word.

A A A a a a   ant ant ant

A A A a a a   ant ant ant

Circle the objects in the picture that begin with the a sound.

Teaching Tips:

Make this lesson interactive by asking questions like:
Is this an apple? Do you like apples? What colour is an apple?
Is it good for health? What is the alligator looking at?
What is the man doing? What does he have in his hand?

A Baked Bun

Trace and write the letters and the word.

B B B b b b   bun bun bun

B B B b b b   bun bun bun

Count the boys and the balloons in the picture. Circle the bottle, the bun and the box.

Teaching Tips:

Make this lesson interactive by asking questions like:
Do you like eating buns? What is the colour of the bun?
What is the colour of balloons? Who is the girl dancing with?

A Colourful Cap

Trace and write the letters and the word.

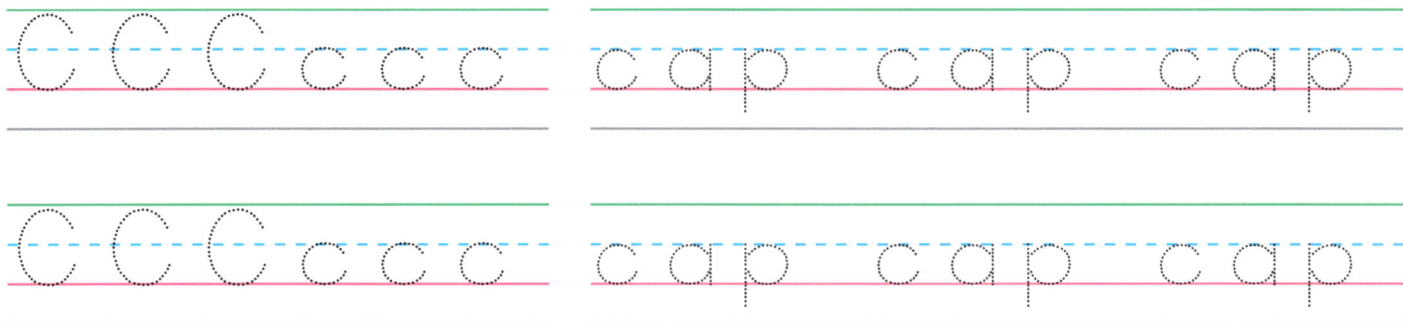

Circle the objects in the picture that begin with the c sound.

Teaching Tips:

Make this lesson interactive by asking questions like:
How many chickens can you see in the picture?
What is on the leaf?
What is the rabbit eating?

A Dainty Duck

Trace and write the letters and the word.

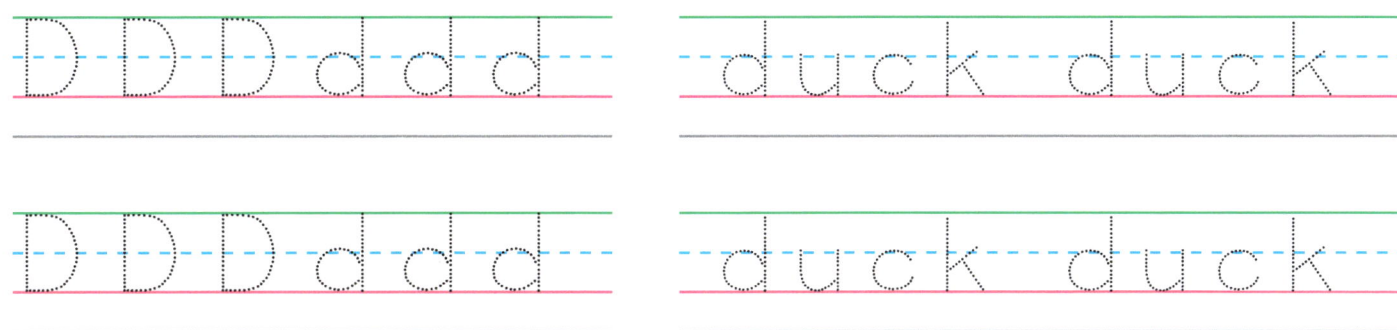

Circle and say the names of the objects in the picture that begin with the **d** sound.

Teaching Tips:

Make this lesson interactive by asking questions like:
Who is in the dump truck? What is the digger doing?
What is flying in the air?

Learn More

Look at each of the pictures below and circle the sound that each picture begins with.

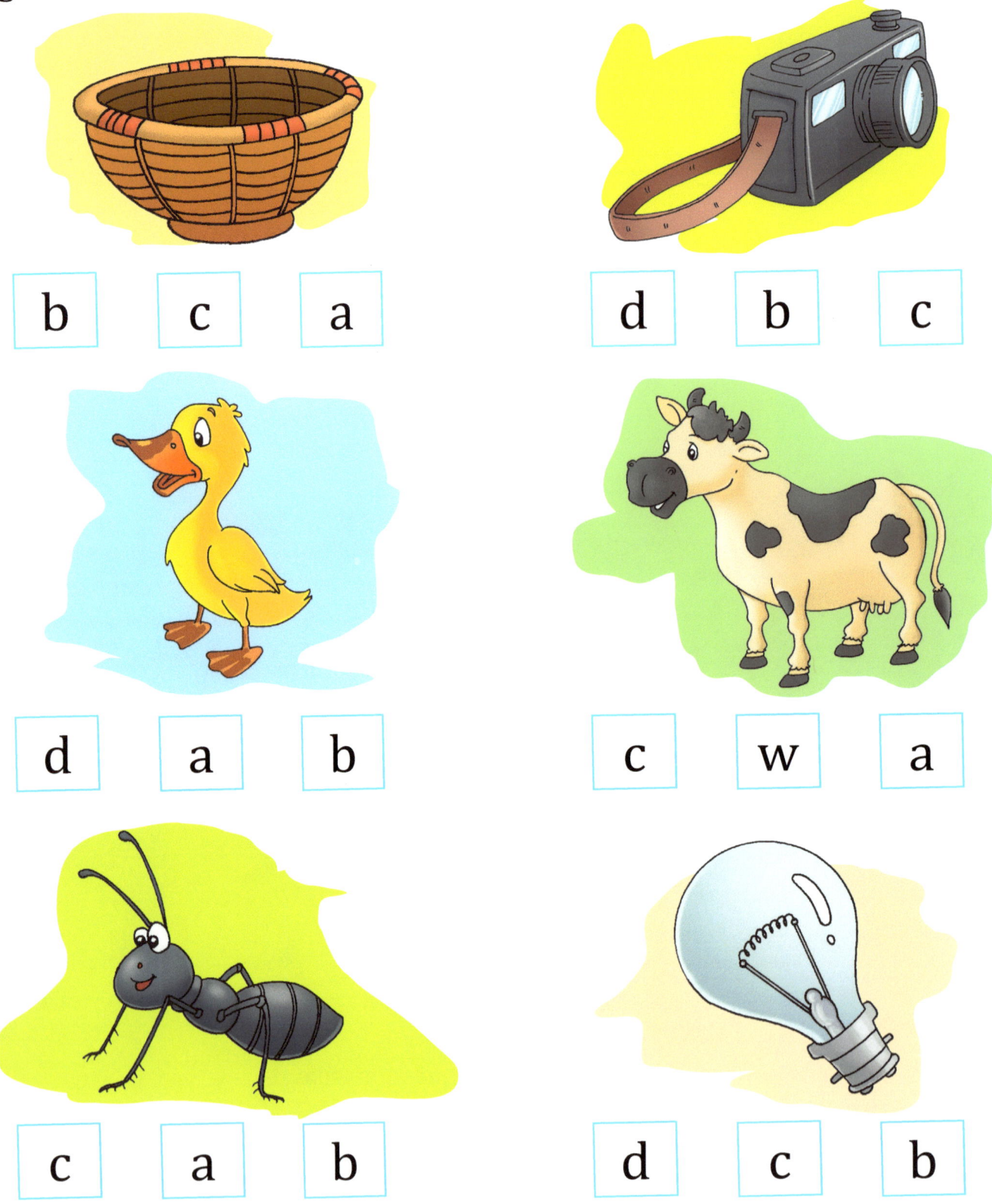

An Easter Egg

Trace and write the letters and the word.

E E E e e e   egg egg egg

E E E e e e   egg egg egg

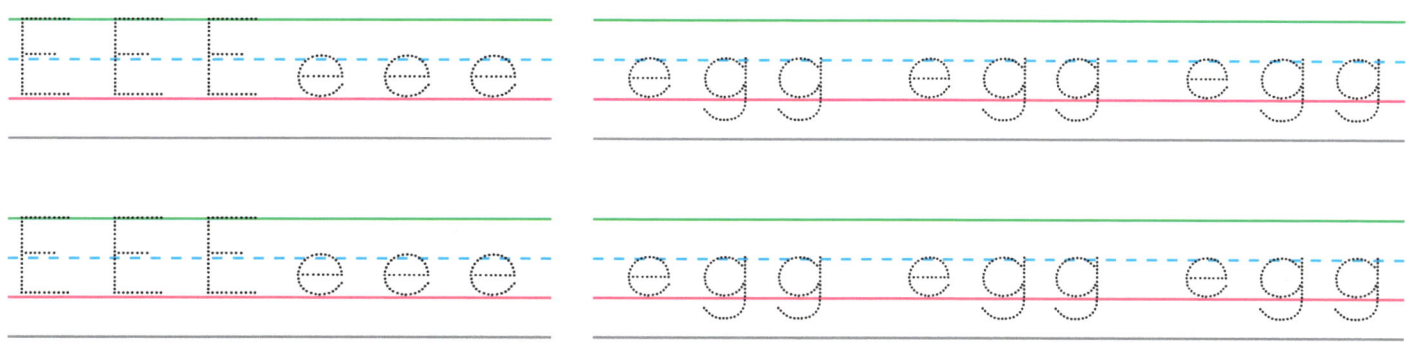

Count the number of eggs in the basket and eagles in the sky.

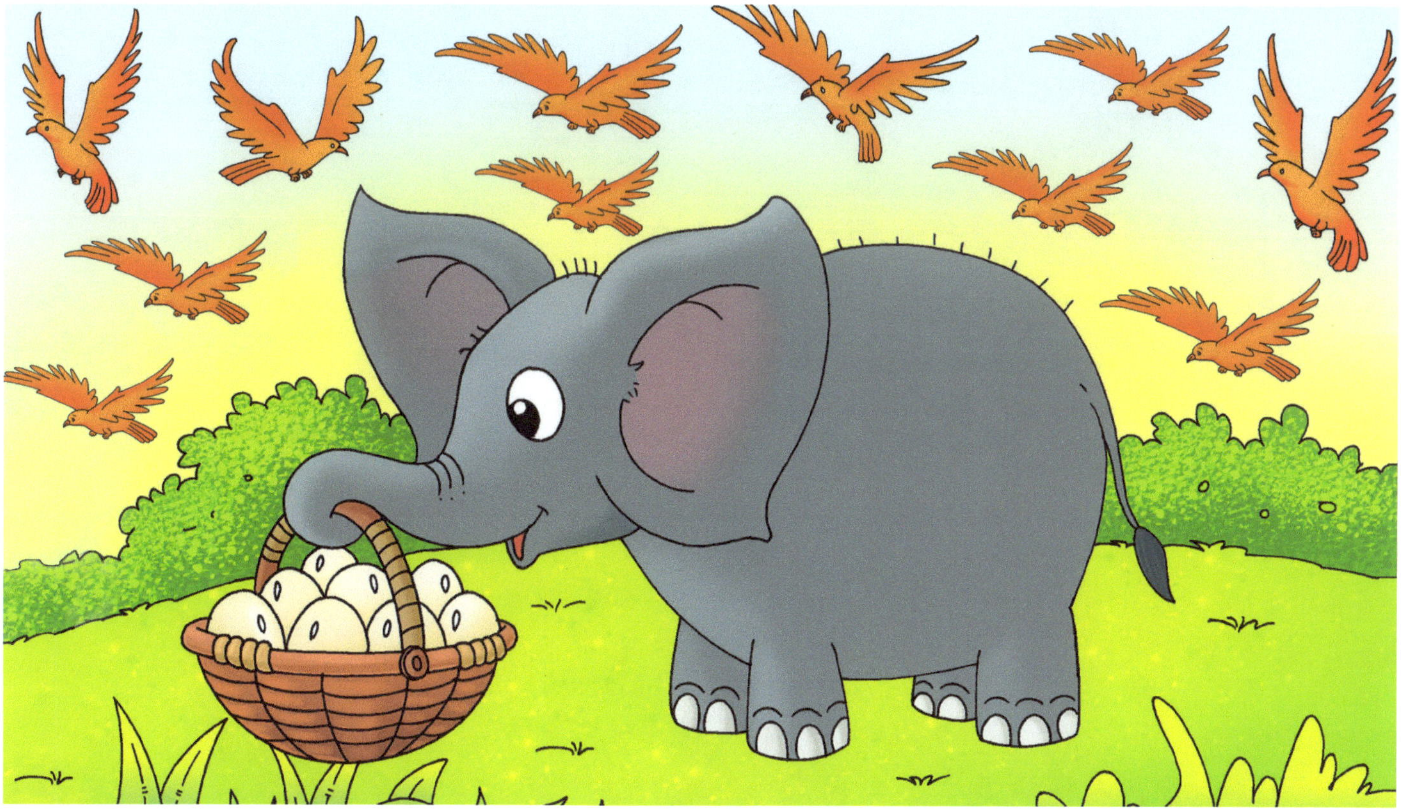

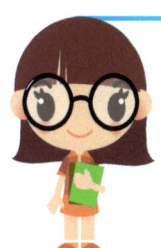

Teaching Tips:

Make this lesson interactive by asking questions like:
Have your ever seen an elephant?
Do you like to eat eggs?

A Foolish Fox

Trace and write the letters and the word.

F F F f f f   fox fox fox

F F F f f f   fox fox fox

Say the names of the objects in the picture that begin with the **f** sound.

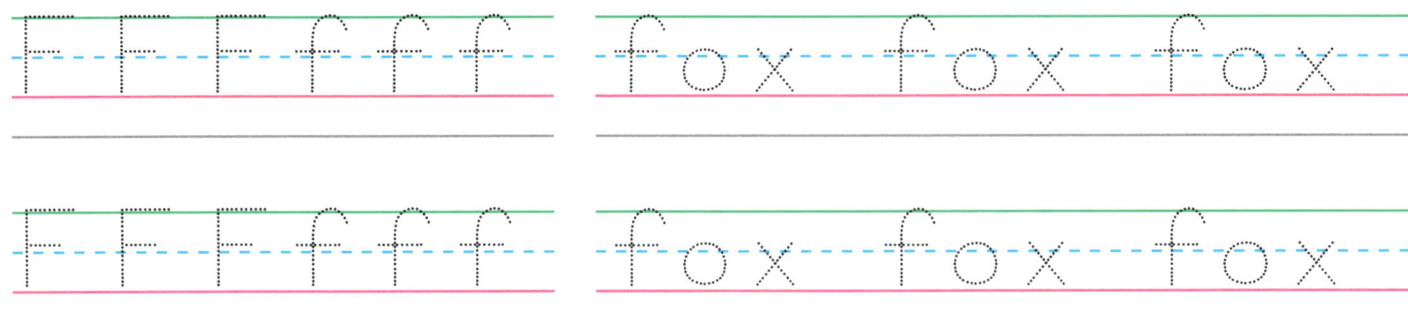

Teaching Tips:

Make this lesson interactive by asking questions like:
Count the number of flies and fishes in the picture.
What is hanging from the ceiling in the picture?

A Good Goat

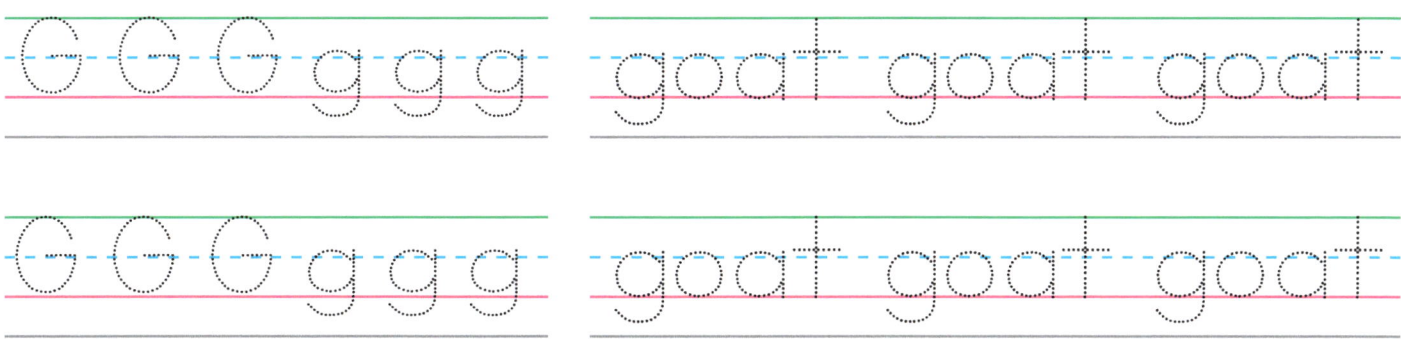

Trace and write the letters and the word.

G G G g g g   goat goat goat

G G G g g g   goat goat goat

Talk about the picture. What are grandfather and grandmother doing? Circle the insect with the g sound.

Teaching Tips:

Make this lesson interactive by asking questions like:
Do you have a garden at home? What do you grow in your garden? What is there on the leaf? What is the colour of the grass?
Can you open the _____ of the garden?

A Happy Hen

Trace and write the letters and the word

HHHhhh   hen hen hen

HHHhhh   hen hen hen

Say the name of the animal that is eating hay. Circle the animal.
Look at the picture of the girl and say the word to complete the sentence.
The girl has long and dark _____.

Teaching Tips:
Make this lesson interactive by discussing about foods that start with the h sound. Ask the children to hop. Ask them to draw a heart and a happy face.

Learn More

Look at the objects in the pictures and say their names. Now say the sound of the first letter for each word and copy it in the space given.

	Elbow	....
	Frog	....
	Guitar	....
	Hammer	....
	Engine	....
	Foot	....

An Icy Igloo

Trace and write the letters and the word.

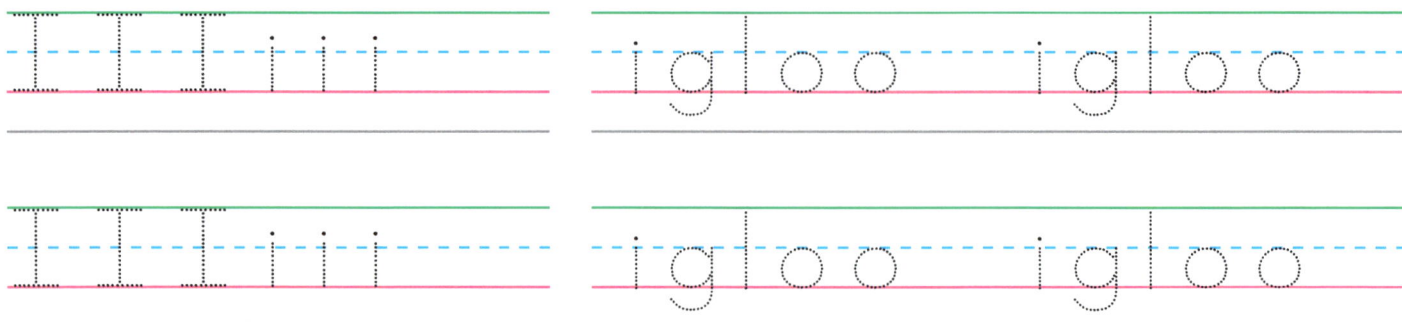

Colour the iguanas green and then colour the picture.

Teaching Tips:

Make this lesson interactive by asking questions like:
Have you ever seen an island?
Have you ever been on an island?
What do islands look like? Where can one find an island?

A Jolly Joey

Trace and write the letters and the word.

J J J jjj   joey joey joey

J J J jjj   joey joey joey

Circle the jeep, the jumping girl and the joker.

Teaching Tips:

Make this lesson interactive by asking questions like:
What is the joker doing? What is the girl doing?
What is your favourite juice? Do you like jam or jelly? Do you know how to juggle balls?

A Kind King

Trace and write the letters and the word.

K K K k k k   king king king

K K K k k k   king king king

Colour the picture and circle the kite, the kingfisher and the kettle.

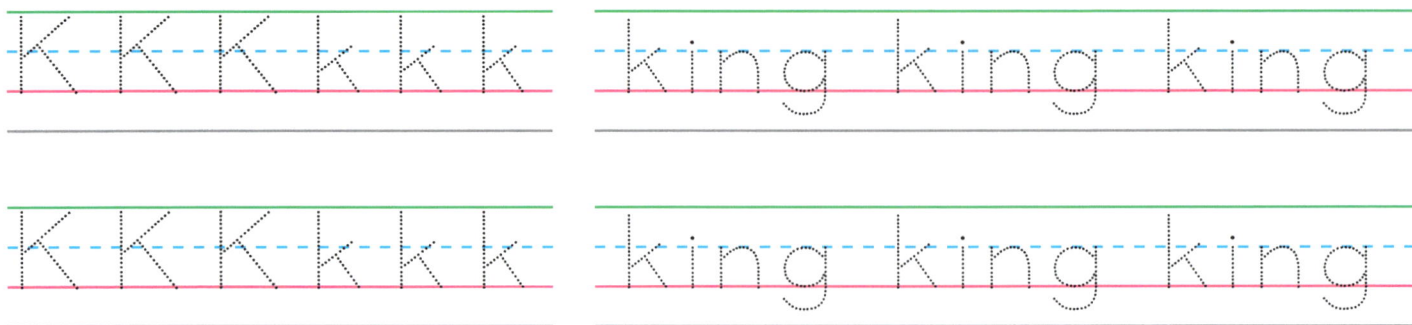

Teaching Tips:

Make this lesson interactive by asking the children to hop like a kangaroo or kick a ball. Ask them to name a few things found in the kitchen.

A Loving Lion

Trace and write the letters and the word.

Circle the lamp and the ladder. Can you spot the lizard in the picture?

Teaching Tips:

Make this lesson interactive by asking children to roar like a lion, lick a lollipop and sing la-la-la.

Learn More

Read aloud the sound and then circle the object whose name begins with the given sound.

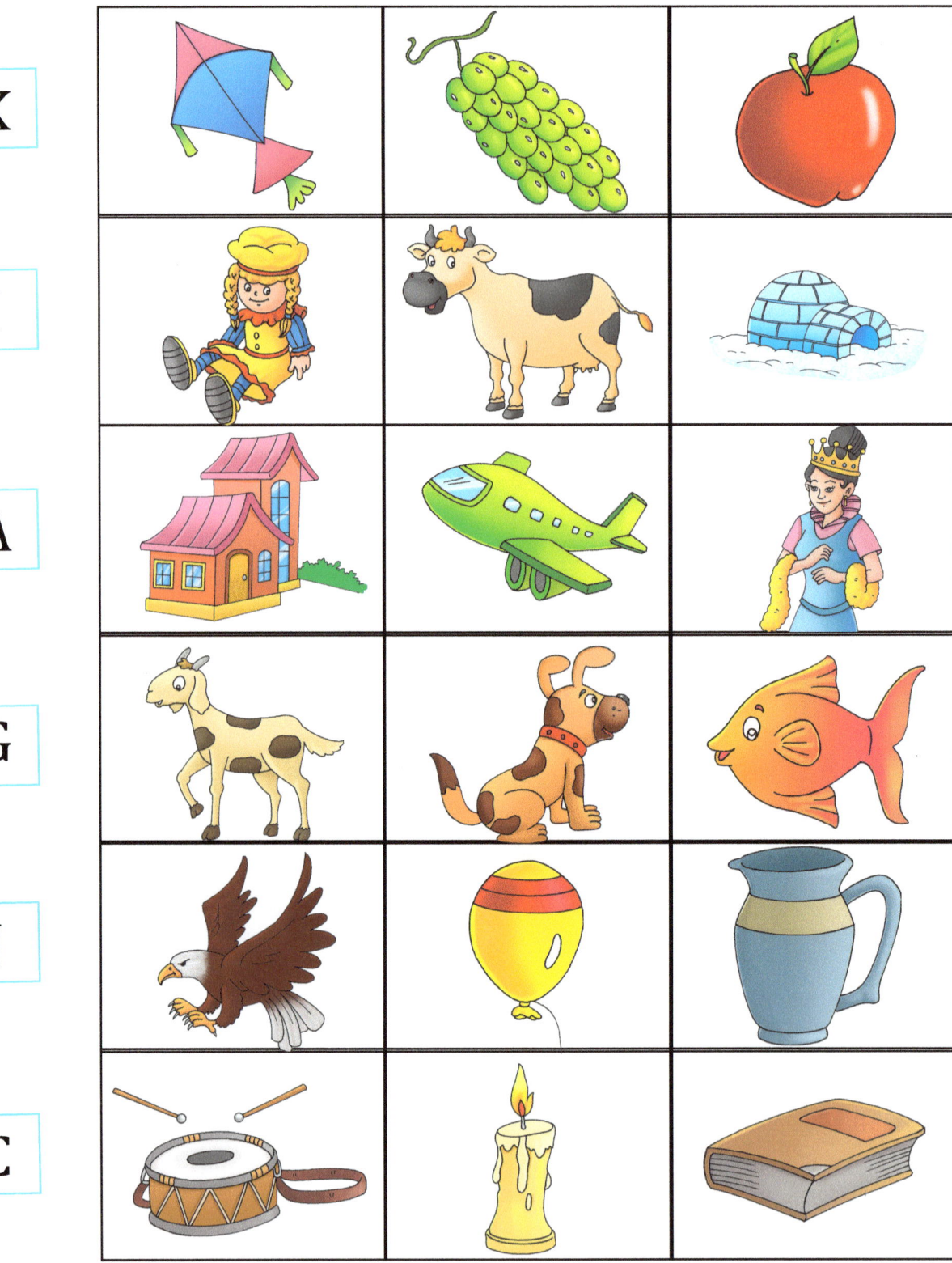

The Magical Moon

Trace and write the letters and the word.

M M M m m m   moon moon

M M M m m m   moon moon

Colour the mountain, the monkey, the man and the mouse.

Teaching Tips:

Make this lesson interactive by asking questions like:
What is the monkey eating in the picture?
What is the man doing?
Why do you think the mouse is digging? Where do mice live?

A Noble Nurse

Trace and write the letters and the word.

N N N n n n   nurse nurse

N N N n n n   nurse nurse

Circle the woman's nose, neck, nails, necklace and the bowl of nuts.

Teaching Tips:
Make this lesson interactive by asking the children to draw a nest. Ask them about animals that live in nests.

20

An Old Owl

Trace and write the letters and the word.

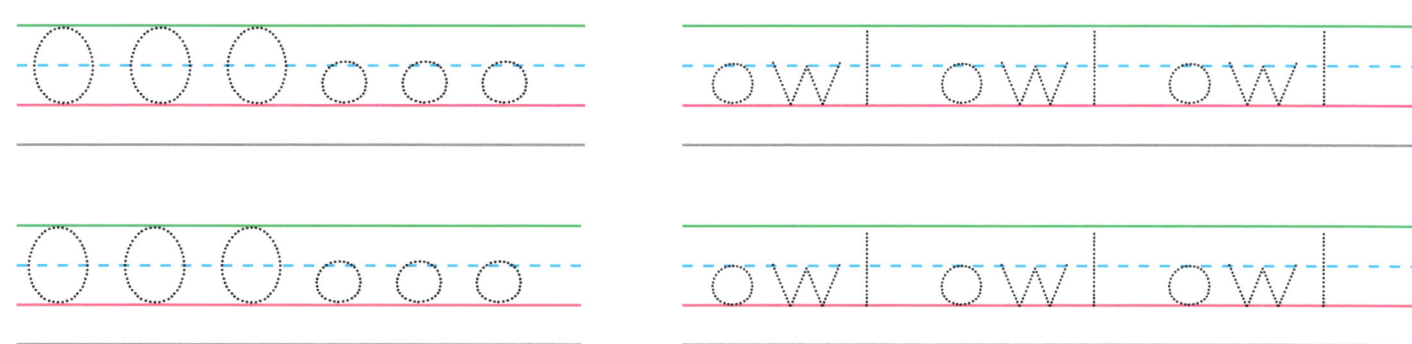

Trace and colour the octopus and the oyster.

Teaching Tips:

Make this lesson interactive by asking the children to sing E-I-E-I-O twice.
Ask them, which is the last sound they hear?
Ask them to sing the rhyme Old MacDonald.

A Playful Pup

Trace and write the letters and the word.

P P P p p p   pup pup pup

P P P p p p   pup pup pup

Colour all the things in the garden that begin with the **p** sound.

Teaching Tips:

Make this lesson interactive by asking the children about penguins and peacocks. Show them pictures of both the birds. Ask them to describe both.

Learn More

Read aloud the sound and then circle the object whose name does not begin with the given sound.

m	monkey	mountains	giraffe
o	owl	apple	orange
p	pineapple	pen	hat
g	house	guitar	gorilla
h	horse	book	horn
n	rocket	nurse	nail

A Quiet Queen

Trace and write the letters and the word.

Q Q Q q q q   queen queen

Q Q Q q q q   queen queen

Circle the quill, the question mark and the quail.

Teaching Tips:
Make this lesson interactive by asking them:
What is a question? Talk about questions. Let them ask questions.

A Red Rose

Trace and write the letters and the word.

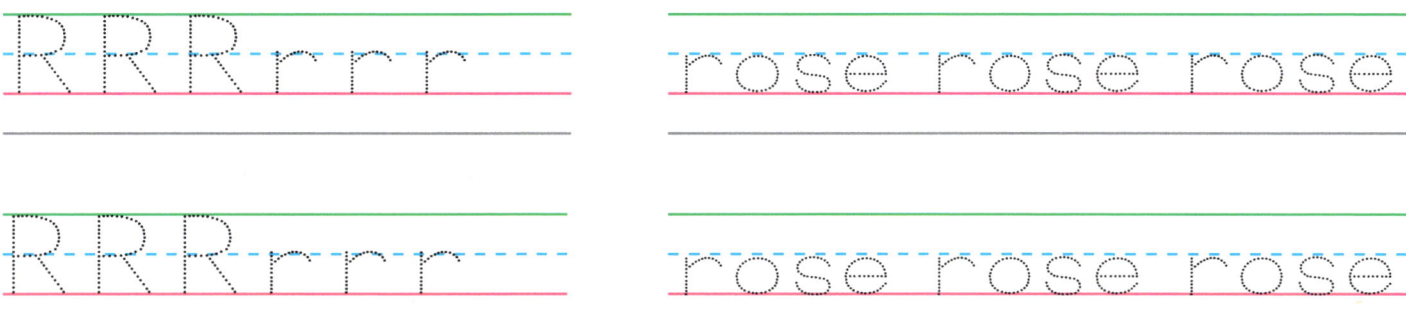

Trace the raindrops and colour the rabbit.

Teaching Tips:

Make this lesson interactive by asking the children about rainbows. Ask them to draw a rainbow and colour it.

Smelly Socks

Trace and write the letters and the word.

S S S s s s   socks socks

S S S s s s   socks socks

Can you spot the sunflowers, the snail, the see-saw and the swing? Colour the picture.

Teaching Tips:

Make this lesson interactive by asking the children to draw snakes in the shape of the letter S.

A Talking Toy

Trace and write the letters and the word.

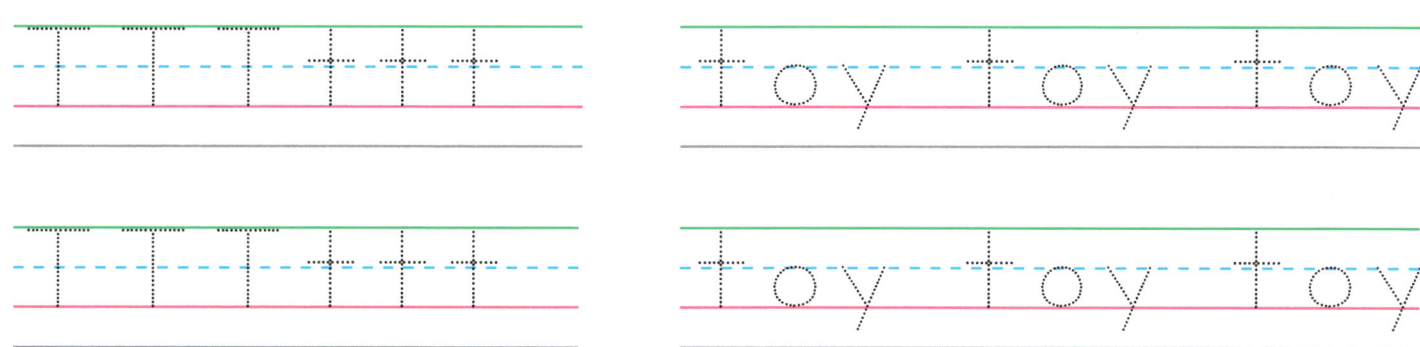

Spot the toothbrushes, the tomatoes, the toy-train, the tent, the teddy bear and the telephone in the picture.

Teaching Tips:

Make this lesson interactive by asking the children to act and show how they brush their teeth.

Learn More

These words have lost their beginning sounds. Write the letter for the sound and complete each word.

[ ] onkey

[ ] itten

[ ] eddy

[ ] ion

[ ] adish

[ ] strich

The Unique Unicorn

Trace and write the letters and the word.

U U U u u u   unicorn

U U U u u u   unicorn

Count the number of umbrellas in the picture.

Teaching Tips:

Make this lesson interesting by asking children to put their arms up. Next, ask them to put their hands under their arms. Ask them to describe the uses of an umbrella.

29

A Vegetable Van

Trace and write the letters and the word.

V V V v v v   van van van

V V V v v v   van van van

What is the boy doing? Can you spot the violin and the vases in the picture?

Teaching Tips:
Make this lesson interactive by asking the children to draw and colour their favourite vegetables.

A Wally Walrus

Trace and write the letters and the word.

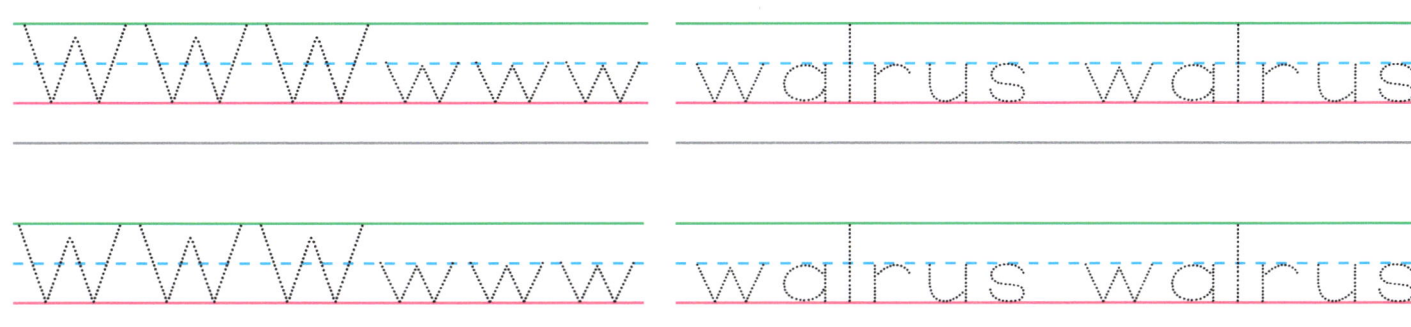

Can you spot the spider? What is the name of the insect flying around? What is the name of the fruit? What else is lying on the table?

Teaching Tips:

Make this lesson interactive by telling children about whales. Show them a picture of a whale and ask them to draw a whale. Tell them stories about whales and whale songs.

A Xylophone

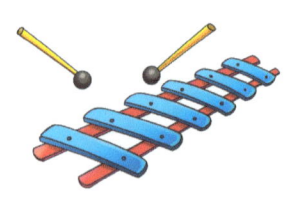

Trace and write the letters and the word.

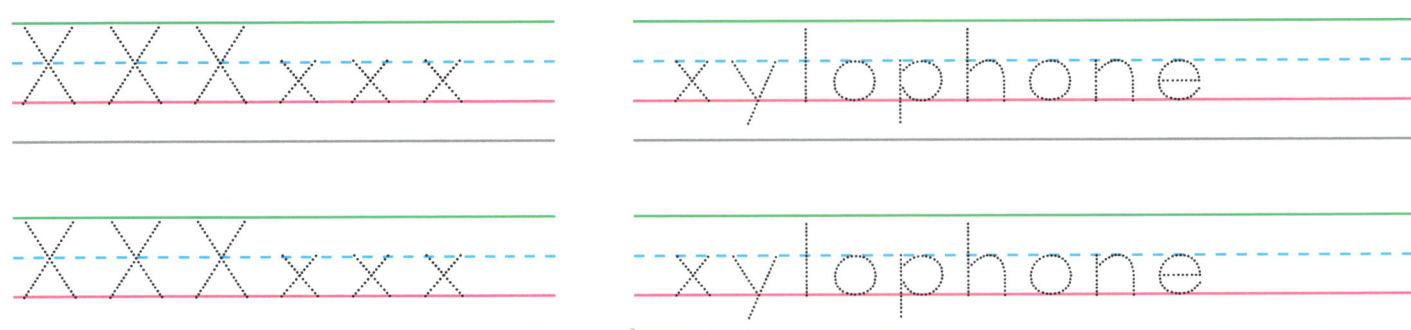

Look at the Xmas tree and its X-ray. Colour and decorate the Xmas tree.

Teaching Tips:
Make this lesson interactive by telling the children to draw a xylophone. Ask them to draw two standing lines opposite each other and then a few sleeping lines across it.

A Yellow Yo-Yo

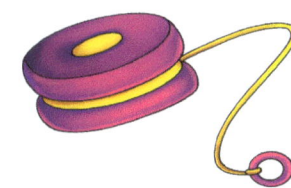

Trace and write the letters and the word.

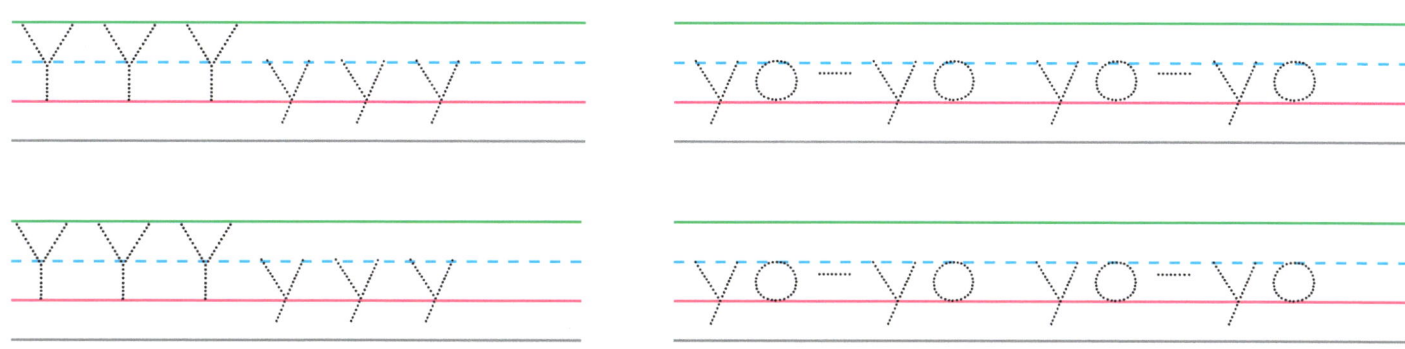

Colour the picture. What is the girl doing? Can you name the animal in the picture?

Teaching Tips:

Make this lesson interactive by asking the children what they do when they are sleepy. Ask them to yawn and show.

A Zesty Zebra

Trace and write the letters and the word.

Colour the picture. Circle the zebra and the zigzag path.

Teaching Tips:
Make this lesson interactive by asking the children to make the letter z with the ice-cream sticks. Ask them to zip up their school bags.

Learn More

Circle the words that begin with the w sound.

What is the train carrying? Can you say the first letter of these objects?

Learn More

Trace and write the words.

yawn

zip

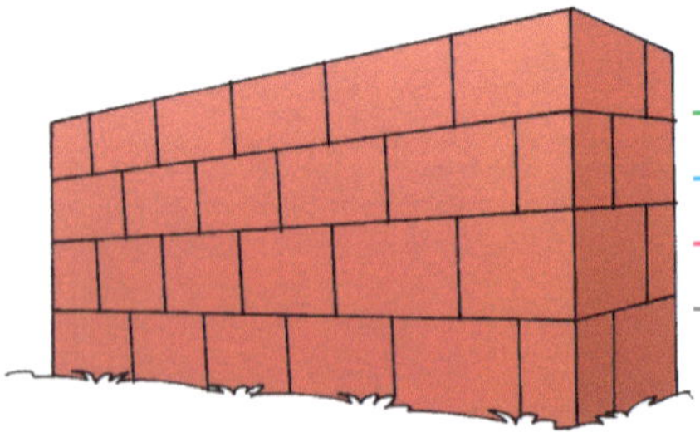

wall

xenops

Draw your favourite vegetables on the plate.

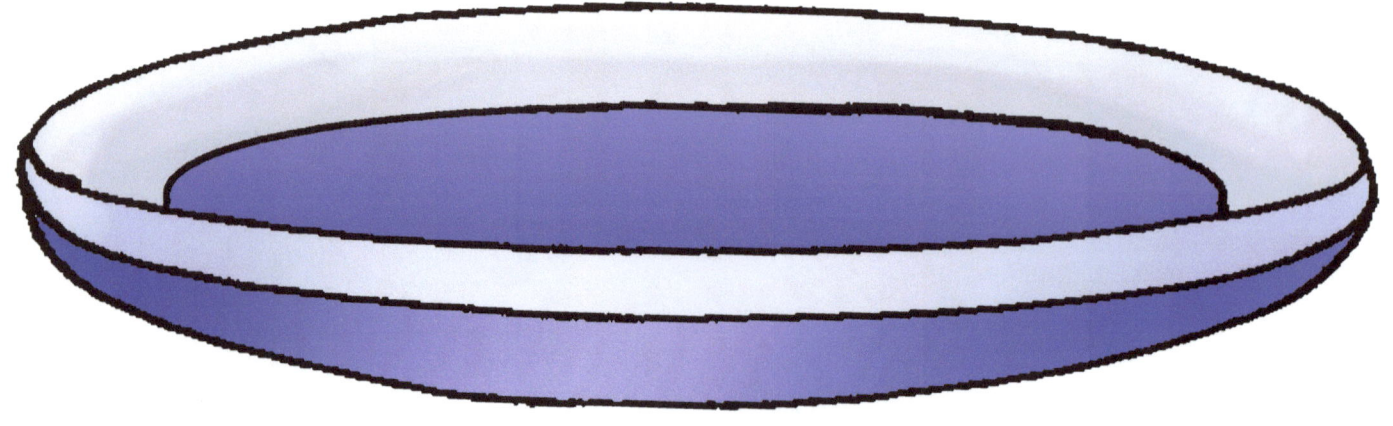

Rhyme Time

Beat, beat, beat the drum,

Dum-badum-badum.

My drum is big and round,

It makes a nice sound.

Dum-badum-badum.

Come, come, everyone,

Playing my drum is lots of fun.

Beat, beat, beat the drum,

Dum-badum-badum.

Matching Fun

Match the upper case letters with the lower case letters. Thereafter match the beginning sound with the correct picture.

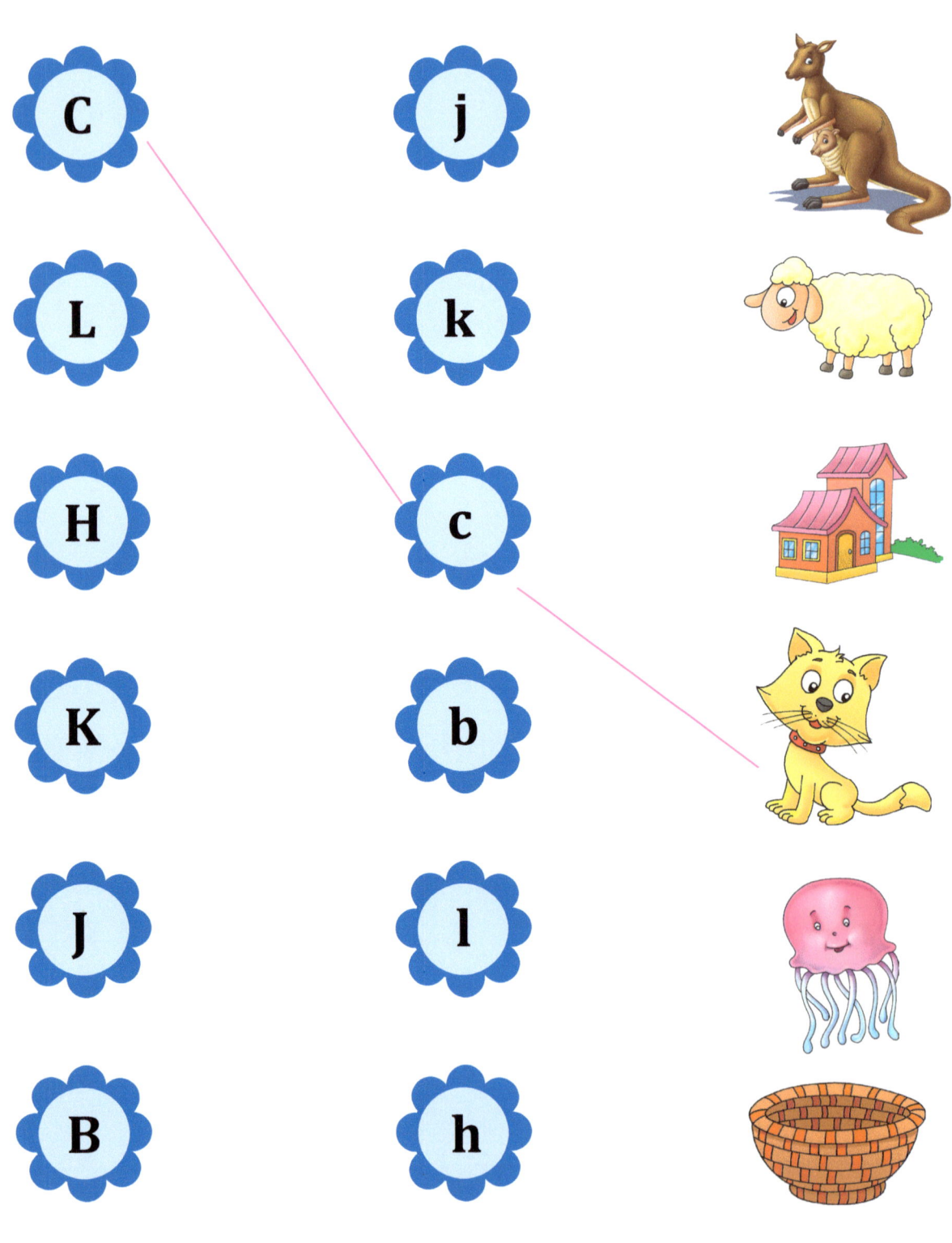

Beginning Letter's Sound

Match the beginning sound with the correct picture.

Beginning Sound

Say the name of the object. Write the beginning sound in the given space.

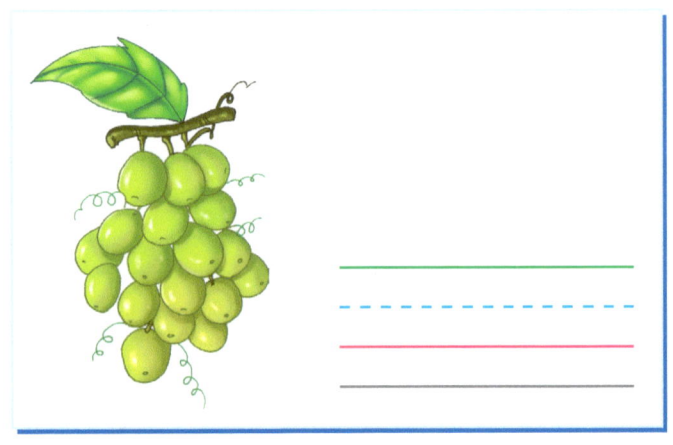

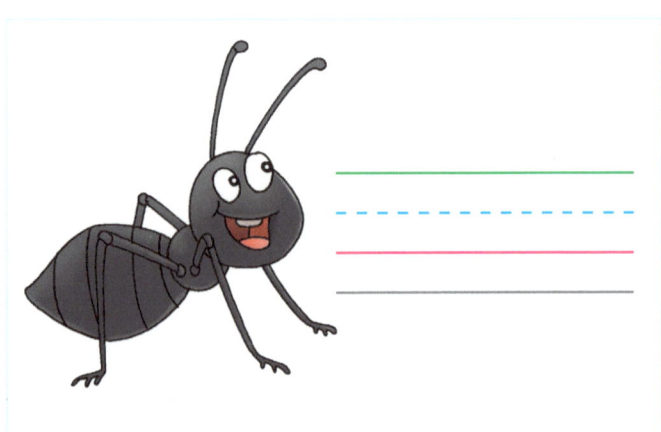

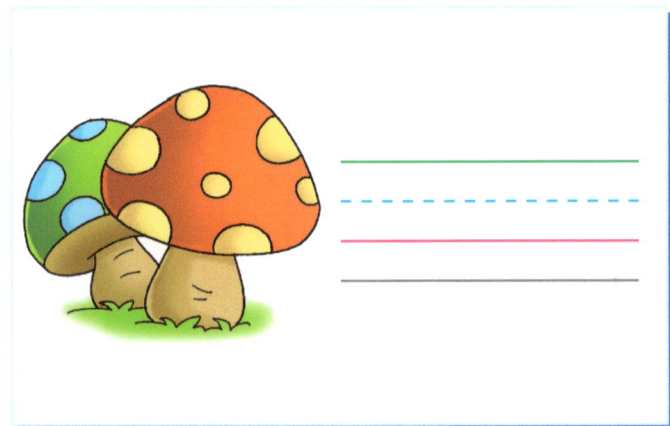

Final Sound

These animals have lost the last letter of their names. Fill in the final letter sound to complete their names.

 Ba ....

 Fo ....

 Ya ....

 Co ....

 Be ....

 Ow ....

Beginning and Final Sounds

Look at the pictures. Fill in the correct letter for the beginning sound of each picture.

......ook　　　......og　　　......ib　　　......et

Look at the pictures. Fill in the correct letter for the final sound of each picture.

Si......　　　　　　Dru......

Cherr......　　　　Lio......

Picture Reading

Here comes the ant named Jill.

Jill lives in an anthill.

This is Tug, the pup.

Tug is sleeping on a rug.

This is Pox, the fox.

Pox likes to sit on the box.

Read and Colour

Colour the clouds blue.

Colour the tree green and the bark brown.

Colour the bird yellow.

Colour the ground green, and the hut brown and red.

Colour the kite with your favourite colour.

Fun at the Zoo

Sam and Pam are going to the zoo. Look at the pictures and write the first letter of each animal in the space given.

..........utterfly   ....amel

..........en   ....ish

..........uck   ....oat

..........orilla   ....nail

..........adybird   ....arrot

Fun with Fruits

Name the fruits. Fill in the blanks with the letters whose sounds you hear at the beginning of their names. Colour the picture.

..........range

..........ig

..........ear

..........anana

..........atermelon

..........rapes

..........ango

..........apaya

Fun with Animals

Fill in the blanks with the correct beginning letter.

1. The ......at is crying.

2. The ......gg has hatched.

3. The ......iraffe is jumping.

4. The ......rog is showing me its tongue.

5. The ......anda is standing on a ball.

6. The ......rab is happy.

7. The ......onkey is smiling.

8. The ......ion is looking at me.

9. The ......at is flying.

10. The ......amel is walking.

Word Ladder

Fill in the missing letters with the help of the picture clues.